The Ultimate 101 Twitter Guide for Marketing Branding and Business

by Neo Monefa

Table of Contents

1. Introduction

In any business, it is important to make your products and services known and available to a large audience and sell them. An important part of getting your target audience to purchase your brand is engaging them continuously. You must build a relationship with them and if you fail to do that then it is safe to assume that no loyalty will be made. Loyalty is important if you want to gain continued support and ultimately, a lifelong customer. There are increasing ways to reach out to your customer and businesses are finding more innovative ways to do just that. After all, in the ever-growing competitiveness of the market today, it is important to learn how to listen to what your customers are saying. More importantly, to not only listen well, but to do it before any of your competing brands do.

One of Social Media's breakthrough roles is in bridging the gap between businesses and consumers. Because of the different online platforms available, the divide between the physical realm and the digital world is made smaller and smaller every single day. Consumers are given a platform to voice out their opinions more than ever. Now, you can hear all kinds of comments about a brand from the good, the bad and the ugly being discussed on a daily level about brands, products, ideas, etc. As conversations about everything and anything—your brand included—propagate on the Web 2.0, businesses need to be extra vigilant. Make no mistake about it, your brand, if not being talked about, is being closely watched.

Twitter is one of the pack leaders in the world of Social Media in terms of the contribution it has made as a marketing tool in the online marketing industry. The interface and the approach of Twitter are simple and easy to use. These characteristics, coupled with innovative marketing Twitter ad products, can result in tremendous way in terms of ROI, awareness or shift in perception, among other things when utilized properly. The brevity of Twitter also forces people to come up with creative ways to get their messages across either through Twitter marketing alone or in combination with other offline efforts. These measures, coupled with your brand's principle messages, are able to penetrate much deeper into your consumers much more than ever before.

Though Twitter may seem like such an easy tool to use, one must recognize the vast power that may be harnessed from this young social media tool. It is important to educate yourself on what Twitter is and what it is actually capable of. After all, if you know the basic principles that build up Twitter and how these can be used in the light of building your brand, amazing results may be achieved. Twitter marks the age of new digital media, and it is a joyful time for anyone who learns how to have fun with its incredible array of opportunities and utilize it properly for business and for growth.

2. The Fundamentals of Twitter

Sharing is the very core of Twitter. Which brings about the question: Why do people share?

People have a natural and psychological compulsion to share. From an early age on, kids at a very young age, as soon as they are able to talk, engage their parents in conversations about what happened to them. This continues on until elementary where kids gravitate towards other kids and friendships are formed on the basis of shared passion for dolls or for coloring books. No matter what the topic, it is safe to say that if people think that it is something worth sharing, they will find a way to share this data.

People share what they can about their lives, about other people's lives, about what they heard on TV or what they read in a magazine. People will share to other people via different communication channels like the telephone, the mobile phone, the Internet, through letters, in person and perhaps even carrier pigeons, if so desired. Whether the content being shared is gossip, whether it's good news or whether it's a great experience, people will find a way to share with other people. It is natural human behavior.

There is this interesting study that came out in Pennsylvania in 2010 that talks about this sharing phenomenon. A group of researchers studied 6 months of data taken from the New York Times among other things. From this research, they were able to deduce the reasons regarding the need of people to buckle down and share certain experiences. Here are the five reasons in bullet points:

- **Sharing tightens shared opinions.** Having someone agree with your point of view will reinforce shared views, build relationships and tighten social bonds. Whether the shared topic is on politics, religion or any key principle or particular industry, the effects are the same. Affinity is built;

a sense of brotherhood is achieved. People will share about their lives in the hopes that someone out there shares the opinion that they have. Tell them to keep a secret and chances are they will end up sharing that too. Here, the saying "birds of the same feather flock together" holds very much true.

•   **Sharing fills the human being's desire to connect.** Human beings are born with the innate need to connect with other humans. The first thing an infant does is instinctively looked for his mother's touch. Why are humans always looking for love? Why is finding a partner one of the biggest life quests? Human beings are wired to be pack animals. In order to get through a situation, humans rely on other humans. This is especially true during times of grief, elation or even when just bored. Humans gravitate towards other people. Human beings have an inherent need to proselytize or that desire to reach out and connect. This can be seen through a variety of situations like causes or even those involved in particular industry such as real estate.

•   **Sharing allows your passion to be known.** If you take a good look at what exactly is being shared you will discover that these can usually be categorized into the following: emotional stories, positive ideas, interesting facts, anger inducing photos, sad songs, etc. Notice anything? Each of these ideas is passion induced. Anything that moves the heart or tugs at the heart strings somewhat are most likely to be shared. This is probably a psychological mechanism that allows humans to temporarily get out of their more boring practical lives in the office. It could be a cry for humanity. It could be going back to your ancestors' times and trying to rouse a sense of the spiritual.

If you can remember the time when email first took off in the early nineties, there were scores of emails circulating about the tragedies about other people. You were required to "send to 10 more people" if you felt the pain or if you "really have a heart". Many people fell for this early version of spam, simply because the story moved them and they had to do as told.

- **Sharing is a great psychological tool to calm people down.** Sharing is a way to soothe your nerves or let go of pent-up emotion. Have you ever felt a lot better after getting a big secret off your chest? Why do you think psychiatrists and psychologists exist? There is a number of people every time anywhere that have things gnawing inside of them. In order to feel better, these things must be released. Sharing is a great communication tool to detox our minds just as vegetables and fruit does to our bodies.

It also helps reduce uncertainty especially during times of disasters and great stress. If you can remember hurricane Irene, communication channels like cellphones, the Internet, radio and television were besieged by people sharing information with each other. Questions like "Does anyone know what to do next?" and "Are you ok?" were thrown around. As you can probably imagine support from the world spilled over as everyone connected and shared on the most basic, human level.

- **Sharing helps to boost confidence and ideas about oneself.** Sharing about a particular experience, a promotion or a new acquisition does a lot in bolstering own sense of self. It's a chance to subtly, or not so subtly drop hints about where you are now in life and your list of achievements. Humans have an inherent need for validation from other people. Humans are used to living by society's standards. A lot of decisions are made based on the question: What will they think of me if I did this? Sharing gives an individual a chance to "boast" a little about himself. For example you won a pair of tickets to a concert, you have a cute new puppy, you got a brand new car... these things are most likely to be shared. It's a chance to validate yourself and see what others may think about you and your piece of news. It also enforces that "I have something and perhaps you don't" kind of human thinking.

What you need to remember is, no matter what, at the end of the day, it will always boil down to this simple truth:

•   **All broadcasting is self-focused.** As a marketer, a brand manager or a CEO of your company, you have to remember that if you are going to create content about your brand and if you're going to share that content, there is always that specific reason why people share that certain content. It is this: that mostly because people as a whole and by nature, want you to think a certain way or a draw up a certain picture about them. Through sharing certain content, they want you to think that they are cool. They want you to think that you are caring. They want you to think that they're funny and smart. They want you to think that they're intellectual and deep.

When you are crafting your tweets and other marketing content for your brand, always remember that golden rule. People will always share content based on this human behavior: the need to validate themselves through other people's eyes. They share based on the principle that "this is a reflection of me and I am aware of that. Because of this persona that I project, people follow me."

3. Enter the World of Twitter

Here is one uncontested truth: Twitter is Big. And it is getting bigger. Here are some statistics to base that claim on:

- As of present, Twitter has a total of 200 million plus registered accounts.
- That is not the end of the story; Twitter gets 600,000 new accounts signing up in a day.
- Over 200 Million tweets get exchanged over the Tweetosphere in a given day.
- Before: to get to a billion tweets, it used to take 3 years, two months and a day. Now: to get to that same amount of tweets, it only takes one week.

If you pause and think about it for one second, that is a lot of information being exchanged in a matter of seconds between hundreds of millions of people. You may also wonder about the type of information that is being exchanged daily. The topics vary greatly. Everything and anything can be discussed on the Twitterverse. There are however some topics that regularly make headway and surface more times than most. Here is a compilation of the most popular subjects that make the rounds daily on this information super-highway.

Twitter's Top 11 Interest Categories

- Celebrity
- Music
- News
- Technology
- Arts and Lifestyle
- Sports
- Humor
- Politics
- Media
- Business
- Non Profit

Twitter Marketing

As you can clearly see, there are a lot of opportunities for you and your brand to make a connection with the number of users and variety of topics. Anywhere here, you can find users who share a point of interest with you, which you can use to your marketing advantage. On a continuous basis, there are conversations going on that have to do or are directly about what you are selling. Twitter marketing is about finding the right place and the methods that you and your brand can employ to find these conversations and jump in. There will always be a category that is relevant to your brand.

What you need to do now is employ some searches. You can use Google, or you can also perform a Twitter search. Here you can find conversations or topics about your brand or at least have something to do with your brand. How you introduce yourself, make your brand known and eventually gain followers is the core of Twitter marketing.

Twitter is Power

What makes Twitter stand out from the rest of the Social Media pie? Twitter is actually a very interesting little tool. The real advantage of Twitter actually has something to do with its limitation. Twitter has a character count. And precisely because it can only contain 140 characters per tweet, the messages tweeted come off as very short, punctual and to the point. There is also the real time nature of its tweets. If you happen to discover something at this moment online or offline, it is very easy to share to the public.

In a matter of 140 characters, you are sharing to your followers and in the digital world different things that you discover. It's very simple and as basic as that. As a result of this ingenuity, you see brand advocates or brand loyalists that surface from the fray. There is also something very interesting that you must know about Twitter followers and how they differ from fans of other social media platforms. Some studies were made regarding the behavior of the sort of people that follow Twitter as compared to another popular social networking site, Facebook.

Here are some examples:

- When it comes to becoming a fan or a follower of your brand, studies show that Twitter users are 67% more likely to be a follower of your brand on Twitter than Facebook.
- Twitter users are also 70% more likely to recommend your brand or product on Twitter.

According to a recent report by research team Forrester, a Twitter follow is not to be taken lightly. This is more than just a button pressed that expresses shallow feelings or a fleeting moment of appreciation. A Twitter follow equals to the most explicit expression of dedication, loyalty and interest to a product or a person online.

Twitter User Demographics

A follow doesn't just mean that you like a certain idea, product, person, brand, etc. It is more than just an existing affinity. A Twitter follow actually increases purchase intent and the willingness to recommend. According to the report on the demographics of Twitter users, as compared to users of Facebook, it was found that Twitter users are more likely to:

- **Be early adopters.** This means that they tend to be advanced when it comes to owning a certain gadget, reading a new book, learning about new ideas, etc.
- **Be more educated.** Whether they have read more or are on a continuous quest to learn more, Twitter users are generally better informed than users of other social media networks.
- **Own a smartphone.** Whether this is because of the combination of the first two points or they simply have more reason to, this was another general trait that arose from the study.

- **Be male.** Although this is a matter that is hugely dependent on the topic being discussed, the studies yielded more male Twitter users generally over other social media platforms.

Twitter as a Purchase Activity Driver

While all these data may seem interesting, what all businesses need to know boils down to one thing. What can Twitter bring to the table in terms of ROI? Will efforts on this online medium generate sales? Essentially, purchase of your brand and ROI is essentially what you want at the end of the day. Is Twitter able to do that? The answer is yes. Twitter has the increasing capacity to do that for social media.

According to recent reports, Twitter drives 56% of people to more likely make a purchase of a brand or product and 59% of people to more likely to recommend a brand than other social media platforms.

4. Twitter vs. Other Social Media

The Follower vs. the Fan

One of the most important things that you must recognize is that social network comments fuel the offline behavior of consumers. The social media network is a very powerful and influential tool that greatly moves people. Whether they buy something or not buys something may directly be the result of what they have been exposed to on a certain Social Media platform. Much like how TV, radio and print in their heyday, had the great capacity to get people out in the streets to buy, buy, buy, social media now holds that ability.

The question now is: Does the particular type of Social Media used impact this behavior greater than most? This is a classic case of quality over quantity as this set of findings from a recent study shows:

Twitter vs. Facebook

Activities that US social network users are more likely to do after they follow a company product on Facebook or Twitter, April 2011:

1. Talk about the company or product
- Twitter: 61%
- Facebook: 49%

2. Recommend the company or product
- Twitter: 59%
- Facebook: 53%

3. Purchase the brand/ company's product
- Twitter: 58%
- Facebook: 53%

4. Link to an ad for the company/ product
- Twitter: 54%
- Facebook: 42%

5. Attend a promotional/ sponsored event
- Twitter: 47%
- Facebook: 34%

By the numbers alone, you can clearly recognize that Twitter users are by far more passionate in their affinity for a certain product or brand. Once you have this set of followers with this kind of affinity and loyalty to your brand, you are on very good ground. Knowing the kind of behavior Twitter users engage in are very good for your brand. And knowing this data, you must begin to find ways for your brand to get involved.

5. Twitter 101

What Makes Twitter Click?

What is it about Twitter that makes it click? What is the very essence of Twitter? If you take Twitter and compare it with other Social Media platforms, you will most probably deduce first and foremost that Twitter's interface is very simple. Once you have joined the Twitter bandwagon and have found yourself tweeting on a regular basis then the answer may have already come to you.

Twitter is really all about connecting you instantaneously with other people regarding your passions and interests on a grander scale. It fulfills that innate need of humans to share and share now. Whether it is an opinion, a new discovery, an emotion or a picture, Twitter allows you to do this on an extremely easy and convenient scale. This differs greatly from other social networks such as Facebook where you purely socialize with your friends and family.

Socializing on Facebook is limited to a set number of people, there is more privacy and the content is not as wide. While Facebook is a tight knit community and used purely for fun and strengthening social ties, Twitter is more wide scale and touches on a more general set of topics. What is important to note is that Twitter is first and foremost deemed as an information network rather than one used for social reasons.

What is a Hash Tag?

Hash tags are a great way to get any number of people together in a discussion about a certain topic, event, idea, etc. Hash tags have the ability to round up all the conversations happening about a certain topic. Here is where you have your audience right where you want them and all you need to do is connect to them. All you have to do in order to start your own hash tag is to think of a clever one liner that does not take too much space. Add a pound sign before your phrase and add it to your tweet. Now, when people want to discuss anything that has to do with your post, they simply look up your hash tag on search engines or Twitter search.

Some examples of how Hash Tags worked in a great way in bringing people together and effecting a significant change in world events include:

• **#Egypt.** This utilized the hash tag in a powerful way that allowed Egyptians to organize a protest against a dictator. It was also the most ideal way for journalists and other media personnel to really find out on a ground level what was going on and discover in real time the events of the protest. Through conversations and information that were tweeted by insiders onsite, the situation was give more depth than clarity than it would have been if otherwise covered and glossed over by news channels. This gave them updates on what was really happening on the ground. This is reality as it happened.

• **#Osama.** This is another great example of how major movements in the Twitterverse were propagated by one simple tweet. This happened to be from an influential person who tweeted about how he was told that Osama has been captured and executed. Tweets with this hash tag: #osama escalated to immense proportions in a matter of minutes. Tweets about how the former dictator's plight escalated to a mad frenzy only dying down at about midnight when people obviously had to get some sleep.

Twitter's Mission

Twitter's mission is simple and that is to: Instantly connect people everywhere to what is most meaningful to them.

With this simple mission, you know your brand can benefit from all the connecting, following and recommending that goes on in the Tweetosphere. Here, Twitter makes known 3 of their ad products that are designed to optimize the marketing of your brand. They are made to complement the great branding or advertising work that you may already have done. When used side by side with your own existing campaigns, you will reach dramatic results for your brand.

6. Twitter Ad Products

1.   Promoted trends. This promotes the most buzz worthy or talked about ad product as of date. It is an ideal tool to seed conversation on behalf of your brand.
2.   Promoted tweets. This is an ideal way to shine a spotlight and draw attention to specific tweets/tweet communications as so much can get lost in the shuffle of the Tweetosphere. You are provided with different mechanisms to bring your tweets and messages more to the surface
3.   Promoted accounts. This is a great tool that you can use in order to grow your follower base as well as your social footprint on Twitter.

Twitter is designed in a way that may solve some of the known problems of Social Media. Each of these ad products is able to perform tasks that effectively complement your marketing efforts on Twitter or offline. Each product enables the optimization of promoting your brand through Twitter.

To take a look at each at greater detail:

Promoted Trends

This ad product will always be found within the trend module. The trend module is Twitter's version of a homepage takeover. It may also be considered as Twitter's redefined version of a homepage takeover. The trend module is live and online for 24 hours. It is also 100% untargeted so that everyone across the globe with an Internet access can see it.

Promoted Tweets

These can exist on your Twitter search or on the Twitter timeline. It is all based on your followers. You get to highlight your Tweet about your product or brand so that anytime anyone searches about a hash tag that you created, your tweet or message will be the first thing that the audiences see. It is the ideal way to keep your important tweet communication from drowning in the sea of Tweets and make sure that your message is properly seen and understood.

Promoted Accounts

This is a great tool that allows you to grow your follower base. It is considered as a paid ad as compared to an organic algorithmic recommendation of your account or as a result of your account coming out in a trending topic. Like a paid ad on, every time that the impression of your account is served, you do not need to pay for that impression. You only pay when someone clicks on your account to follow you. It keeps you visible in the market, so to speak.

These new ad products from Twitter are unlike anything that you will see in the digital world or real world. Each of these products serve a specific purpose and when used in combination with other marketing efforts can yield truly powerful results for your brand. The more traditional ways of digital marketing or advertising is long gone. This is the new frontier. If you are not convinced, ask yourself when you last clicked on a banner. Simply put, these ad products are redefining the way social media marketing is done. It

It changes how companies now embark on digital marketing and it has yet to see anything similar to its platform. Through these Ad Products used in Twitter, brands are starting to reach tremendous results in terms of raising awareness and generating sales.

7. The Twitter Equation

To give you an idea of just how wide and huge Twitter's reach can be when utilized fully by brands, take a look at the following statistics:

The Top Five Winning Tweets in May 2014
- VW = 52%
- Google = 38%
- Old spice = 36%
- Ford = 34%
- Papa John's = 34%

These numbers are huge comprising almost a third of the entire Twitterverse, which as you already know is at hundreds of millions and still growing. What is even more amazing is how you can use Twitter alongside your existing offline marketing efforts. To further understand this theory, see how Twitter is in fact, impacting the offline world.

Twitter and the TV

- **Twitter is changing TV.** Cable and network providers love Twitter because Twitter is able to bring in more viewers to them. This ultimately results in higher revenue for these cable networks and channels.

- **Viewers love Twitter.** Twitter in many ways has become an entirely different screen experience for them. Here they can share their thoughts about certain TV shows, build up on ideas or have their questions answered. It is a virtual community hub where fans of the same show can get together and start conversations.

The whole notion of a shared viewing experience is present in Twitter, much like having watched a movie together and discussing it afterwards.

What Can Twitter Do For You?

Here is something you may want to ask yourself: Just how big can a brand get through Twitter? Here are some examples to answer that question:

- At the Superbowl, tweets per second reached up to 4,064 at the very peak.
- Audi integrated the hash tag at the end of their TV spot: #progress. As a result, they were able to enjoy a huge TV size engagement through their ads and through Twitter as well. They purchased a promoted trend so that their tweet comes out first when you search #progress. All the resulting tweets for #progress skyrocketed as a result of joining forces between online and offline marketing integrations.

Obviously, Audi must have done something right by marrying online (Twitter) and offline (TV) platforms. The campaign was an amazing success leading to record first quarter volumes for their cars.

Twitter Strategy

The Twitter strategy is the product of years of careful experimentations and studies, which were developed side by side with SalesForce. As a brand who may want to work with Twitter and Salesforce you will most likely be encouraged to try out Promoted accounts and Promoted tweets. These will make up the most fundamental cores of your brand's Twitter campaign. Why is this so? The answer is simple. If you have anyone who is searching for your brand, as how it is with the existing principles of search engines, you want to shine a larger spotlight on your promoted tweet.

That way, to this searcher, it is your tweet or message that comes out first. Remember, you have a very qualified and well-defined user searching for your brand and you must do whatever you can to take advantage of this search. That having said, Promoted accounts and Tweets are two very effective green light approaches you to employ with your Twitter marketing strategy.

Promoted Trends is also very important because it is live during a 24-hour period. It is also typically at a higher price point than the other Ad products so this is best used to leverage campaigns with for bigger events like product announcements, big marketing activities and other such things of that scale.

8. Case Studies

Case Study 1: Discovery Channel

An example of how this ad product was utilized effectively is through Discovery Channel. The channel wanted to draw massive attention to and attract greater viewership and audience to one of their new landmark series: The Curiosity Project. By effectively seeding conversations about episodes of The Curiosity Project, people were brought together, discussing the topics of the series. The first subject matter dealt with for that series was God and the universe. Discovery channel seeded questions, debate topics and the like about God and the universe and opened up channels of communications between a wide reach of audiences.

Case Study 2: Old Spice

What is truly amazing about Twitter is that there is a tremendous amount of influence or pull involved in the platform. You may be surprised at the number of celebrities and key people in all major aspects of the world who are registered Tweet users. One such example is Kevin Rose, the American entrepreneur who is the founder of Digg, Pownce and Milk among others. Kevin is a huge deal on Twitter. He has a commanding seven figure footprint on Twitter.

Old Spice makes use of his incredible pull and integrates him into their Old Spice YouTube ads. Kevin Rose then tweets about his involvement, thereby reaching his millions of followers. The effect, as you can guess is tremendous. When a truly commanding influence like Kevin of Digg interacts with your ads, you can be sure that all of a sudden, conversations about Old Spice and its ad spikes. Now you have tremendous traffic to the YouTube ad and you have people talking about the ad not only on YouTube but also on Twitter.

Because of Kevin Rose broadcasting his involvement with the ad and essentially with Old Spice as a brand his 1.2 million followers are instantly reached. That is not to say the number of re-tweets that this may initiate. It is a mindboggling figure to even imagine.

Case Study 3: Coca-Cola

This also works for brands, which have been around for a long time, even considered legendary. For the simple purpose of reinforcing affinity or strong brand loyalty, take this for an example. One of the most iconic brands of all time is CocaCola, which also happens to be one of the early partners of Twitter. They created a Tweet by Doctor Pemberton—the man who invented the Coca-Cola. He is known as @docpemberton. This is his tweet:

"I'd like to raise a glass (of Coke) to all those who love and drink my invention."
#youdeserveashoutout

The tweet did not offer an accompanying landing page or a URL that Coca-Cola wanted to promote. It was simply about starting and owning a delightful and nostalgic conversation. Having someone as legendary as the inventor of Coca-Cola raise a glass to all the millions of Coca-Cola followers out there is a big deal. As you can imagine, the hash tag #youdeserveashoutout propagated the Tweetosphere for several days. It is a classic example of making use of an iconic brand and marrying it with new digital marketing ad products from Twitter.

Case Study 4: Xbox

Promoted account is an awesome tool for your brand or company to grow your existing follower base. It is especially helpful in the light of new information that you want to share. It has become a powerful tactic for a lot of brands both big and small to make use of prior a grand announcement such as a product launch. An example from Xbox back in 2010 clearly shows this example.

Before the company launched their new product "Connect", they leveraged their marketing efforts with Promoted Accounts on Twitter. What they were able t do was grow their pool of followers in time for the big day. This ultimately drew more attention to the grand launching day, which happened on November 4.

Case Study 5: RadioShack

Another great case study of the utilization of promoted accounts is from RadioShack. For many years, RadioShack has been known as the destination where you can purchase cords, extension cords and other products of similar nature. Well, they wanted to break that notion. What they did was turn to Twitter marketing to help shift that perception to something else. More than anything and when used correctly, Twitter is all about being a brand building tool.

So when RadioShack wanted to be known more for cellphones, they purchased a promoted trend for a period of 24 hours. Along with a catchy hash tag, they also employed the influence of some celebrities. When Lance Armstrong tweeted under the #uneedanewphone, the tweets and retweets in that subject category skyrocketed and effectively resulted in awareness and ROI for Radio Shack in the days that followed.

Ad Age Digital published the following statement following the RadioShack marketing efforts on Twitter using Promoted Trends:

"RadioShack saw wireless platform sales increase double digits in the three days that followed the promoted trend the ROI on this social media initiative was stratospheric for us."
– CMO of RadioShack Lee Applebaum

What is most exciting to note is that brands are finally reaping ROI from online marketing and advertising efforts like never before. While there was a gap between the real world and the digital world before Twitter, there are suddenly new ways wherein these digital advertising moves can directly lead to generated sales. Twitter is finally marrying that great divide between the physical world and the digital world.

Suffice to say, that aside from the increased awareness about RadioShack and the shift of perception as to their reputation, there was also huge amounts of in-store traffic to their stores in the period of their campaign. Guess what, there were also incremental sales of their cellphones.

Case Study 6: VW

Here is an example of a brand yielding a massive amount of engagement by using Twitter marketing. They capitalized on the very popular subject matter of music. VW decided to make use of the biggest music festival in Brazil called the Planeta Terra in Sao Paulo and display their new car model "The Fox" in there. VW saw this as an excellent opportunity to bring the young fans of the concert closer to their trendy car The Fox.

The question that the VW Twitter marketing specialists asked was this:

How do we let the rest of Sao Paulo know that the Fox would be at the Planeta Terra?

First, they pointed out that they needed to hear by creating #FoxatPlanetaTerra. Then they offered them something that they wanted: tickets for the festival. The twist? They made it not-so-easy to get those tickets, and this is what truly added fire to the campaign. VW decided to hide these tickets in 10 different places within the city of Sao Paulo. In order to find the hidden tickets, people had to tweet #foxatplanetaterra. The clue was an aerial snapshot of the hidden city taken from miles away. The mechanics were simple: the more tweets, the closer the zoom of the hidden city gets as displayed on their landing page.

The first one to arrive to the hidden city won a pair of tickets. A few minutes later, another race begins. This campaign went on for 4 days straight. And the effects were tremendous. There were different ways to bring the zoom closer through the simple act of tweeting. There were users calling upon other users, there were those who simply added the hash tag to their regular daily tweets. Within days, Sao Paulo was the trending topic on Twitter, which reached VW's intended audience which was Sao Paulo. The VW campaign was a phenomenal way to utilize Twitter in a fun and engaging manner for the young target audience.

140 Characters Can Move the World

It doesn't take much to move the world. Apparently, 140 characters is all it takes. When done right, utilized correctly and in combination with other forms of marketing, advertising and PR, Twitter can harness amazing results for your brand. The true essence of Twitter lies in the massive amounts of creativity you are forced to employ given the character limitation.

It is this creativity along with the brevity of Twitter that impacts change. This is not only true for advertising or marketing campaigns. Major movements in the political and cultural landscapes in North Africa, Egypt, Indonesia and Libya have already felt the power that can be harnessed through Twitter. Twitter can shake up the world. Imagine what it can do for your brand.

9. Twitter FAQS

1. Does Twitter share the demographic data to the brand or company?

Yes, Twitter shares all the demographic information obtained through the use of the platform and its products. What can be said about the Twitter demographics right now is this: massive amounts of strength lie in the 18 – 34 age demographic.

When your brand decides to use Twitter for your marketing or advertising processes, you are able to break down your followers by area as well. You will get clear data and percentage breakdown of audiences that are coming from the US and the specific states within and those that are coming from Germany, Canada or Indonesia for example.

When you have the actual twitter program and the analytics contained within, you are able dive deep into your followers' demographics. You get full access of their data. These analytics, dashboards, statistics and other data become available to your brand when you start to utilize promoted products on Twitter.

2. What is the best way to craft a Tweet?

Salesforce struggled with this question when it first got into Twitter. It started off doing more of the traditional PR branding style when they first created their accounts. This is because this is what PR typically did and Salesforce only copied them. As time went on, they decided to do some experimentation with the way they handled their Tweets. They took a persona that they looked up to and mimicked the way he spoke.

Suddenly Salesforce started to sound comedic and sarcastic. When this voice started coming out people sat up and took notice. It is good to try and make people think to themselves: "Hey. His brain is different. I want to get to know more about this person."

People started to tweet them and Salesforce always tweeted back. One thing you must remember is that no matter how great or funny or smart your Twitter brand is, it will all be in vain if you fail to engage in conversation with your followers. You must take time out to tweet them back.

When you validate someone's voice or presence, you are engaging them and make them feel special. This is an essential cornerstone in building your brand and building brand loyalty. For any brand, it is important to try and focus on creating engaging moments. If you are only starting out on Twitter and are still looking for your voice, go ahead and start with what you know. Now if this doesn't work or you don't get the results that you would like, then it is time to start experimenting.

The best thing about social media is that there is no one formula or recipe for success. It is always changing and evolving along with the times. The only real rule is that you stick to your own voice and to your own instincts. Remember, the best recipe is the recipe that you make. In other words, there is no right or wrong Twitter method. There will be differences between each one but you can't really say that one is better than the other. What is important is that you find a strategy that works for you and stick to it until it is time to revolutionize once again.

You have to find your own voice when it comes to tweets. This can only come from experimentation and perhaps some stumbles along the way. Also remember that when you sell that voice internally to your company's executives, you must say that "look this is an experiment. It may work, it may not work." But never put your foot down and state that "This is it. This is our voice." Because once you do and this voice doesn't work, then you have nowhere else to go. So make room for mistakes, go on an experimentation phase, learn from it and grow from there.

3. Is there a link between Twitter and another popular social media platform YouTube?

There are incredible lengths concerning the link between twitter and YouTube. Twitter is able to drive tremendous amounts of traffic to YouTube. Actually, most of Twitter's promoted products do a massive job in driving scores of traffic to YouTube.

The Old Spice campaign example is only one of the promoted products that was able to generate a large amount of traffic to YouTube. This was a result either directly or indirectly care of people re-tweeting those particular ads. You are also easily able to embed a YouTube video in your tweet on occasions when you want your followers to see a video directly and right away. Simply take the URL of the video and paste it on your tweet box. Because of these conveniences, Twitter has become an ideal broadcast tool where it opens up other social media platforms to the users.

Twitter also works with a number of video providers and live stream providers such as Livestream.com and Ustream.com in order for the user to have enhanced experiences on Twitter and vice versa.

4. How does Twitter work with a teen audience?

Twitter has a teen audience. The best way to optimize marketing to this audience is to find ways to dive offline as well to start really promoting your brand creatively with this audience. As with most aspects of marketing, it is all about testing, learning and jumping right in. As long as you have your company's core messages that you want to employ, you can work around with that. It is best to start off with these basic building blocks and then just start integrating more fun pieces of content along the way to fully engage with the teens.

5. What are other strategies to help you engage an audience?

Twitter is first and foremost, a brand building tool so this must be kept in mind as the core principle of this social media tool. You want to find out the words that your influencers are using. The lingo that they are making popular with their followers, what hash tags they are using. Next, create Twitter searches for those hash tags so that when those conversations appear, you jump into those conversations and make yourself known. It is important to let people know that you're there. The best way to do that is to say that you are not exactly sure what you are doing there but that you would like to learn about this and that.

And you will be surprised at how simply asking for some help will do amazing things for your brand. Also, learn to think about how while Twitter is a great broadcast tool for a lot of individuals it serves as a great dialog tool as well. Despite followers only waiting to hear tweets from their favorite celebrities, they can actually engage in conversation with them. You not only are given the chance to create a conversation with your audience but also with your peers.

Once you start thinking along those lines, you will see that an incredible amount of creative opportunity opens itself up to you.

6. Any secrets to boosting a certain hash tag or the visibility of promoted products?

There are some best ways to inject or boost a hash tag or the visibility of promoted products but these things come to you at different points of your experimentation. You will eventually find out why some hash tags get greater prominence on the web more than others. Reasons for this differ. You will learn that it is not all about the number of conversations that happen around that specific hash tag. Although that is part of the equation, it is also the velocity or the speed of how these particular hash tags are being propagated through Twitter.

7. What is the use of the TweetDeck?

While TweetDeck is an amazing tool, you may be surprised to know that most executives use twitter.com. They don't use the TweetDeck or other platforms similar to it. These are usually reserved for the individuals who are wearing multiple hats in a company. TweetDeck is best used by those who are tweeting in behalf of multiple handles for a company.

But please don't rule out those platforms or tools completely. Simply find out how best you can use them if need be because they are excellently capable of engaging multiple loads of tweets in a more efficient manner.

8.   Is there any significant difference between the male and the female tweeter?

Yes, there are some differences. Some studies show that females have the tendency to tweet incrementally more than males. Females can tweet and re-tweet for a number of reasons. They may be following some mom-related content or going through mommy websites if they are a mom. This does not mean that their tweets are limited to this category though. They may also have their tweets about a personal interest such as around celebrities, fashion or around news.

There are no real massive or obvious trends at this point between males and females since a lot of it is subjective. While it is true that mommy conversations tend to drive more within the female community than jet engine manufacturers, you will see that a lot of it is from an anecdotal standpoint. This is usually happening in a community manager chat social where they set aside an hour out of each day. They make an announcement that in this hour, we will talk about these three questions and then provide a hash tag.

As someone trying to track down female Twitter users you can try and use that hash tag to track down relevant conversations to your brand. So when you actually find those conversations and jump in on, you can get a lot of information. This information coming from your peers or colleagues from other companies who are interested in the same things becomes an excellent wealth or resources.
So, is it true that women are more active or less than the male? It still really depends on the subject.

9. How to get the most impact out of every tweet?

First it is important to really think out your strategies well. You must know that to get more friends or followers is not what you want.

What is important is to find the right buyers. It's a classic case of quality over quantity. You must seriously look for these people who are joining a particular conversation because here is your mine of users who have a need that you can fulfill.

What you need to do is get serious about Twitter marketing. You must make an effort to hire someone to go out there, collect the data and analyze them well. That someone must find out where all these important conversations are happening. If not, you need to have someone from the company to buckle down and make it their job to find these conversations. There are plenty of options for this. You can even hire an agency or work with one of the specialists from Twitter. These guys can help you figure out how to do searches related to your company's particular needs.

Again, you must find someone to locate the conversations relevant to your brand and happening around your space and jump right in. Here is the thing about social network that you must know. It is not all about broadcasting what you want and waiting for everyone to start coming to you. That is not how it works. You, as a marketer, must really know how to get out there and make contact. You really have to engage. That is part of being a social networker. You have to go out of your way and talk to people, ask questions, build affinity and develop that rapport.

That is where the real strength of social networking comes in; the fact that you're creating a brand moment.

Here is a message about brands from Bruce Campbell, the Chief Message Officer for Salesforce. He has done campaigns for Pepsi and Nike among other brands.

The brand is not the logo. It is much more than the colors or the font or the image. It goes deeper than pure physical and aesthetics. The brand is in each and every single moment that they have an experience with the brand. Whatever this moment is with this brand is what they will always remember. For example, maybe someone bought a certain pair of shoes because he remembers that one time in middle school track practice that the guy who beat him up was wearing a pair of Nikes. And he thought to himself, "Well if I had a pair of Nikes, I'm going to wear them!"

This thought maybe got stuck in his head and that is why they want a Nike. The brand is the moment, the memory. How that particular something made you feel at a particular moment in your life. And that is what you want to create for your audience. It is creating that positive reinforcement with them. First of all, that your brand cares, that the brand is listening and finally, that you are human. Pin down those concepts and that's more than half of the battle won right there. Remember, simply throwing out a message and hoping that everyone will come round is simply not going to work.

10. Any advice for a small start-up business that wants to utilize Twitter?

First and foremost, you need to remember that you don't want to simply grow your following. A growth in following should be a result of engaging. People should follow you because of the example that you have set with your previous followers. It is not about blindly attracting followers. Most of it has to do with the quality of your followers.

Again, the best way to find your followers and serves as a great learning component for your business as well is to find other people or other businesses that are in your space. You want to start engaging them in conversations. Maybe you can find community managers who start discussions around a certain hash tag. Maybe your business can even start your own hash tag because your competitors are most likely following you. So you would like to engage them in discussion and get what you can get out of them.

Maybe the first time you go and try to do it you will have five people participating in your discussions. The next time you do it try and shoot for ten. Before you know it your numbers will grow incrementally but that is not going to happen overnight.

As a start up is your goal to build awareness for your product, generate interest in your company and in your products and maybe steadily build your followers.

The first thing you can do is to engage your peers. You must start pairing up with the people that you meet in conferences, events and congregations like these. These are essentially the people that you exchange your business cards with. This will start off their awareness of your product or brand. So that when you do get to the point of launch your product or your new service, you have a core group to support you. They will be the ones who are most likely to tweet about your product, share about what your product is all about or how beneficial it is. It is every important to build rapport with your peer group or network.

Second part is if you want to sell something, you have to change gears and really go out there. You must prepare to launch a real Twitter campaign using a combination of offline and online efforts. A way you can also do this is to search for a product where you can find your competitors at and cherry pick them. You can set up searches for people who are looking ideas, experiences with ideas to exchange with your competing brand. Once you do, you check out the conversations happening and jump in.

Jumping in Conversations

People in these conversations may not be happy about a particular service or product, be alert for these particular areas. They may say that it costs too much, or not enough information is provided or I don't know how to set it up. Any kind of feedback is crucial at this stage. Then, join these conversations based on what you read. Simply say that you noticed that they were having some problems with this certain brand that you just happen to have some experience with it. How can you help? You will be surprised at the sheer number of people that would start talking to you.

Gain their sympathy and don't try to bring up that you have a competing product straight up. It is always better to offers some help first and foremost. Here is your chance to point them out to resources that will aid in their problem. They will usually discover on their own that you work for a competing brand or maybe in time you will tell them yourself but do not tell this to them straight up. It is always ideal to be causal about these things and have a real conversation with them first. Ask questions, show that you care and take it from there.

11. Who can do the job of Twitter Marketing the best?

A lot of companies make the big mistake of talking to the young new hire and asking them to do the job. They think that because he is young then he is automatically part this new digital culture. This is one of the worst things you can do. Remember that in any industry, your best marketing move is and always will be knowledge. Whoever knows the most about the company, whoever knows the most about the product should be the one answering the questions. Put anyone who knows less and you are in big trouble.

Of course this individual may not know how to speak in "Twitternese" but here is where you can find ways to rectify that. You can pair him up with someone who knows more about the medium, you can send him out to a crash course or to some classes, or teach him the basics like how to craft a 140 character tweet and take it from there.

Again, the best marketing folks will always be the ones who have the right answer at the right time of need. Once you are able to put that kind of person for the job at hand, you are certain to win in your marketing efforts every single time.

10. Conclusion

- **Be honest with your tweets.** Have fun with what you are doing. No matter what, don't try to sell anything to anybody. It goes without saying that the Twitter audience is a lot smarter than you think. Anything you say that is pretentious will be sniffed out. Be as natural as you can when you post and yes, being too forward with your marketing messages will only turn off your audience.

- **Try to be funny, catchy and informative.** You don't have to be all three at the same time at all times. Sometimes two out of three isn't bad. What is important is that you put some effort into your tweets. A halfhearted tweet is nothing more than a waste of space in the Twitterverse.

- **Twitter about things that have to do with your brand, but also Twitter some things that have absolutely nothing to do with it.** Widen your universe. You don't to stay within a set of pre-determined topics. The best thing about Twitter is the vastness of the opportunities. Think about all the untapped potentials floating around somewhere. If you play your cards right you have the potential to tap into them and make them followers.

- **Share interesting links, share original or inspired ideas, ask funny questions, answer questions you know the answer to, do any of these except "what are you doing?" unless what you are doing is really, really interesting.** 140 characters is a small space to waste on a tired old cliché of answering what you are doing. Put this as a tweet and chances are it will barely make a blip into the world of Twitterverse. Use every chance you can to show everyone out there how incredibly charming/ smart/ original you are.

- **No matter how brilliant your posts are, you must get out there, get active and follow others.** Make use of this great tool available to you for tossing around ideas and connecting with not only your peers but with some of the greatest minds in the industry. Great things are not borne out of lurking and staying quiet. You must get out there and create something.

- **Join the conversations.** There are so many interesting ones happening. Don't be one of those Twitter users who simply use the platform to promote your product or services. It is self-serving and boring.

- **Take time out and really think about what you are going to tweet**. Write each and every word like it matters, because in Twitterverse where you only get 140 characters, it does.

- Think about it. Every time you send out a tweet, you get a chance to say something about your brand. Don't blow it on trivial, unoriginal and boring things. Because Twitter is free to use, many take advantage of this. What they don't know is that it costs them more to have uninspired content.

- **If you run out of ideas, think about things that matter to you and share them**. You can share interesting links. You can share your insights on a particular topic, you can share new trends you chance upon, or things that are significant or new.

It helps to be personal and to have your own voice. The trick here is to keep yourself visible in the Twitterverse. It is important to let your followers know you are there, expressing yourself and sharing stuff that is relevant. At the same time, do not overdo it by over-Tweeting about yourself and your services. This may have you marked as spam and have your account removed.

In a nutshell, Twitter really is about discovering new things about others and more importantly, about yourself. You can treat it as a way to learn more about your brand and gain new insight like never before. The process of self-discovery is always fresh, exciting and new. Don't be discouraged by failures and the little obstacles that slow your progress instead, take these chances to grow your brand and become stronger. Let Twitter allow you to become a better version of your brand. That is, after all, what you are put here for.